THE FABRIC OF US

POEMS ON TRUST, FAMILY, AND LOVE

ADITYA SINGH

I am grateful for the friendships that became family, the relationships that shaped my heart, and the college experiences that shaped my tale. This book is dedicated to you, with thanks and love.

Contents

Foreword

College is a transformative period in our lives, a time of discovery, growth, and unforgettable experiences. It is a journey marked by the friendships we forge, the love we encounter, and the myriad of moments that leave an indelible imprint on our hearts. In this collection, I have woven together the tapestry of my college years, capturing the essence of the people and events that shaped me during this pivotal time.

These poems are more than simply words on a page; they are glimpses into my soul, reflections on the joys and struggles, laughter and sorrow that accompanied me during those formative years. Each poem is a picture, a clear remembrance of the events that shaped my college years. From late-night chats and shared secrets with friends to the bittersweet complexity of love, this book pays homage to the lively and often turbulent path of youth.

As you read these pages, I encourage you to walk with me through the halls of my college, to sit with me under the ancient oak tree where I found consolation, to experience the excitement of fresh beginnings and the agony of unavoidable goodbyes. I hope my words strike a chord with you, eliciting memories and feelings while also reminding you of the universality of our experiences.

This book is dedicated to those who have shared this journey with me, to the friends who have become family, and to the loves who have taught me about the depths of my own heart. Thank you for taking part in my tale.

May these poems serve as a reminder that even in the smallest moments, there is beauty and meaning to be found.

With heartfelt gratitude,

ADITYA SINGH

1. Whispers of Deceit

In shadows of the heart, a tale unfolds,
Of love unrequited, a story of old.
I cherished you, my heart in your command,
Yet you slipped away like grains of sand.
Your smiles, a glimpse of heaven's grace,
But truth concealed in every stolen embrace.
I cared for you, a love so deep and true,
While in your heart, another love you knew.
Betrayed by whispered lies and secret kisses,
In your embrace, I found my heart's misses.
You painted promises with brushes of deceit,
In this tangled web, love's bitter and sweet.
A fleeting touch, a kiss upon your lips,
It once felt real, now memory's eclipse.
You swore you cared, no other held your heart,
But the pages of our love have torn apart.
Now history's ink has dried upon the page,
A story of love that time cannot assuage.
I'll learn to heal, to find my love anew,
For my heart still beats, in search of love that's true.

2. Unveiling Deceit: A Journey to True Love

In the chambers of my heart, a story unfolds,
Of a love that burned, while your heart remained cold.
I cared for you, a flame that never waned,
But you, in deceit, another's love obtained.
Your promises were petals, delicate, untrue,
A mask that hid the depths of what you'd do.
I held your hand, believing every word,
As in the shadows, your betrayal stirred.
You kissed him, as you once kissed me so sweet,
A moment in time when two paths did meet.
But your lies were the dagger that cut so deep,
While I, in blindness, your secrets couldn't keep.
I gave my all, my love so pure and rare,
While you, in falsehood, danced without a care.
In the chapters of our tale, I found my pain,
Yet I'll rise above the storm, love's bitter rain.
For love is not measured in the tears we shed,
But in the strength to move on, to heal instead.
In your unrequited love, I'll find my way,
To a brighter, truer love, a brand-new day.
Though you never loved me back, it's time to part,
To mend this wounded heart, to restart.
The rest is history, a chapter in the past,
I'll find a love that's real, and make it last.

3. Pages of Love: A Library's Embrace

In the quiet of a library's embrace we met,
Two souls converging, destiny's sweet duet.
A girl with laughter, a sparkle in her eyes,
Together, we shared dreams 'neath quiet skies.
With books and projects, we dived into the day,
Creativity sparked in our unique way.
In the library's hush, our ideas took flight,
As we stitched together stories, bathed in soft light.
The world outside faded as we worked side by side,
Lost in our visions, on this joyous ride.
The magic of laughter, the warmth in your smile,
Made the hours pass swiftly, mile by mile.
As the sun dipped low, painting skies with grace,
We transitioned to the evening's warm embrace.
A movie's gentle glow, and you by my side,
Our hearts whispered secrets, nothing to hide.
But amidst these memories, one thing stands apart,
The magic in your eyes, the gateway to your heart.
A depth and mystery, I couldn't look away,
In those endless pools, my thoughts wished to stay.
Though chaos may have followed, a tempest in its wake,
Our journey had moments, no mistake to forsake.
And while time might pass, and life's currents may part,
I hold those dear memories close to my heart.

For even in the storm, the heartache, and strife,
I'll cherish those moments that defined our life.
In the library's soft hush, and by the movie's warm glow,
A connection we found, a feeling I'll always know.

4. Fractured Bonds: When Love's Sky Darkened

In the shadow of a once-sunlit sky,
Our love, once clear, began to mystify.
A single day when storm clouds gathered near,
The echoes of our first fight still clear.
We argued fiercely, words like daggers flew,
About what we were, what our love might construe.
Were we just friends, or something more profound?
In the chaos of it all, our love unwound.
In the beginning, hearts beat in harmony,
But as time passed, they played a different melody.
Emotions that once burned like a blazing fire,
Now flickered, dimmed, extinguishing desire.
A crack appeared, fragile like fine glass,
And through it came a presence, an unwelcome trespass.
A boy, a stranger, slipped into the divide,
And in that fateful moment, my heart ached, sighed.
I knew in that instant, the pain was far too clever,
Our connection severed, lost now and forever.
The fight that day etched a line we couldn't mend,
Our love's story forever altered, without an end.
As I look back, those memories do haunt,
The day our love withered, the day we'll never confront.
"Fractured Bonds," a tale of love's cruel endeavor,
A heart once whole, now broken, shattered, forever.

5. Promises Unfulfilled

In the tapestry of time, I saw a face,
A girl whose presence filled my heart's embrace.
I gazed into those eyes, where futures danced,
And in that moment, destiny's seed was advanced.
I told her, "With you, my dreams take flight,
A future together, so pure and bright.
A small family, love's journey to commence,
I'll handle your moods, with patience immense."
"I love your imperfections," I confessed with grace,
"I want to hold your hand in life's endless embrace.
Through old age's wisdom, through every storm we'd weather,
In your eyes, I'd find home, in us, I'd find forever."
Her response, a smile, those words she'd convey,
"The most beautiful thing," she'd gently say.
But alas, the tides of fate can be so unkind,
And now, the echoes of her memory haunt my mind.
For I was the one who loved her unconditionally,
Through messy behavior, and her lack of organization, so free.
I believed in her when others could not see,
In every situation, her strength was what I'd see.
But a shadow, a tiger, came to steal my dreams,
Ripped apart our plans, shattered love's seams.
In an instant, the future I had envisioned,
Lay in ruins, crushed, and harshly imprisoned.
I might be the best person she'd ever know,

The love I had for her, in my heart would glow.
But life's cruel twists, its turns and strife,
Made me just another figure in her life.
Promises unfulfilled, a love that's lost,
In the wake of this tempest, at such a cost.
The memories linger, bittersweet in their view,
A love that was deep, a future that never grew.

6. Fading Echoes of A Broken Bond

In the pages of time, a chapter unfolds,
A tale of two hearts, their stories once told.
I remember a moment, a vivid refrain,
When sickness stole you, and you bore the pain.
You had to journey back, to the home you held dear,
In those quiet rooms, where sickness and rest drew near.
And though our words fell silent, as you slept through the day,
The memory of your absence refused to fade away.
"Impatiently, I longed for you," was your heartfelt plea,
"Baat kar na mere se," you said, a balm to me.
Voice notes, like love notes, with your sweet voice they came,
A source of comfort, like a gentle, soothing flame.
Your voice, a melody that played in my ear,
A lullaby of love, casting aside all fear.
As healing found you and your strength was regained,
The love we shared grew, the bond was maintained.
One Thursday, you returned, an unexpected sight,
A surprise that took my heart, soaring in flight.
Yet now, our connection, our once steadfast tether,
Frayed and broken, a bond we'd now sever.
For twenty-five days, we've walked this desolate shore,
Fifteen days of silence, a void we could ignore.
Your indecision, a chasm too wide to bridge,
The love we shared, now a wounded ridge.

The scars you left, deep and profound,

No salve can heal, no solace can be found.

Though I once longed to hold you, to take you back,

Now, in the echoes of our past, I've lost track.

"Fading Echoes of a Broken Bond," our story's sad end,

A love that was cherished, now lost around the bend.

Too late to mend the pieces, too late to restore,

The love we once had, now a memory no more.

7. Whispers of love lost

In days of yore, in love's sweet light,
There dwelt a girl, a precious sight.
Her eyes, a sea of endless grace,
Could steal the breath from any place.
Her smile, a radiant work of art,
Could mend the cracks of any heart.
Her voice, a melodious song so sweet,
Made the world's chaos feel complete.
Though stature small, in love we'd bind,
Our souls, our hearts, entwined, entwined.
The way we'd hug, so close, so tight,
Her ears near my chest, in the night.
But sadly, in this love's cruel game,
She couldn't hear my heart's true flame.
My silent words, my yearning plea,
Remained unheard, forever free.
She said my kiss was hers alone,
Yet lips that strayed, my love bemoaned.
My friends, they warned, they tried to steer,
But in my heart, you were still dear.
In the end, we lost our way,
Our love's enchantment began to fray.
Now I stand in a better place,
With a friend's warm embrace.
You needn't care, for I am free,

No longer bound by what could be.
I hope you find the love you seek,
In another's eyes, so bright and meek.
May happiness be your guiding star,
And true love find you, near or far.
I wish you joy, a love that's true,
But one thing's sure, I'll always love you.

8. A friend's unending light

In life's darkest hours, when shadows loomed,
I found a friend, my heart's embrace, assumed.
She was the one who walked beside,
Supporting me, in my tempestuous ride.
Her scolding words, like tears in eyes,
Were lessons learned, a precious prize.
In my mistakes, she'd guide my way,
With love and care, come what may.
When I gazed into her eyes so deep,
My worries fled, as if in sleep.
The world would fade, our souls connect,
In moments cherished, I'd reflect.
She disliked the pictures I took with care,
Yet, in her heart, I knew she'd wear.
A smile that's meant for just my eyes,
Our friendship's bond, no sweet disguise.
I prayed to God, with all my might,
To keep her happy, every day and night.
To shield her from troubles, life's cruel chore,
And guide her to a brighter shore.
I don't believe in a love that's forever,
But in my heart, our bond will sever,
I'll care, I'll love, I'll scold, I'll guide,
Till the end of time, by your side.
I hope you find someone who cares so deep,

And through your craziness, their love will seep.

To all the world, your beauty's known,

But in your soul, I've truly grown.

A promise I make, forever true,

I'll always speak honestly to you.

No matter how bitter the truth may be,

I'll cherish our friendship eternally.

9. A Soul Reborn

Today's the day, a newfound dawn,
Where happiness within me is reborn.
My laughter echoes, just as before,
My old smile, like a river, to explore.
Lost it was, with the girl's deceit,
But now it's back, oh, so sweet.
For I was searching, the stars above,
But forgot I too, shine with love.
In the peace I've found, my soul's delight,
I see my life, once hidden from sight.
Mistakes I've made, but I understand,
From my window, I pen this, with an open hand.
From here, I journey, no turning back,
Not to old love, nor friendships that lack.
But with my family, I'll stand tall,
In their love and embrace, I'll give my all.
A soul reborn, with lessons learned,
In the gentle breeze, my spirit churned.
No longer lost, I've found my way,
In this new chapter, I'll seize the day.

10. A Day of Joy and Emotions Unfurled

In the morning , with my bestie by my side,

A day of joy, together, we'd confide,

We set forth, on this journey to be,

A day of laughter, and memories set free.

With classmates, we gathered, a merry band,

Laughter, and chatter, we hand in hand,

We embarked to delete the past's old frame,

In the warmth of friendship, we'd stake our claim.

With the sun high above, we hung about,

Under its golden rays, there was no doubt,

Our spirits soared, as if on wings of a dove,

With every moment, we found, more to love.

As the day unfurled, like a vibrant bloom,

We faced the future, leaving behind the gloom,

The evening came, with a gentle, cool breeze,

A time of reflection, beneath swaying trees.

The evening walk, a heartfelt talk for me,

Amidst nature's embrace, under the twilight's decree,

The best conversation, I'd ever had,

With friends so dear, it made my heart glad.

For I know, these days won't always remain,

In the pages of time, they'll dissolve like rain,

But in my poems, I'll etch them with grace,

To hold on to these moments, in life's hectic pace.

When sorrow and darkness try to pull me down,
I'll reach for my verses, banishing the frown,
For in those lines, I'll find the light,
To lift my spirits high, in the darkest night.
So cherish these days of joy and delight,
For in the warmth of friendship, everything's right,
Let's capture these emotions in our heart's embrace,
So they'll shine as guiding stars, in life's boundless space.

11. An Angel's Grace

In the realm of life, a fleeting chance,
Two months ago, fate's charming dance,
I met a girl, a rare find, it's true,
Her essence, a radiant, shimmering hue.
Caring and mature, her heart's pure gold,
A treasure to cherish, a story yet untold,
Never did I dream, such a soul exists,
In her warmth and wisdom, my heart persists.
Her explanations, like magic, they unfold,
In her words, a world of wonders, untold,
I thank the heavens for this gift so divine,
A companion in happiness, in sorrow's line.
We share our days, in the gym we sweat,
Through trials and triumphs, we haven't met,
I pray to the skies, for the man she seeks,
To treat her with kindness, for the love she speaks.
Beauty she wears, not in pride, but grace,
Down to earth, in every step and every pace,
Her attire, a testament to her refined taste,
In her presence, I find solace, a sacred space.
The future's unknown, where it may lead,
Through battles and arguments, we may indeed,
I pledge not to wound, to be forever near,
In your joy, in your sorrow, my presence clear.
In the chapters unwritten, together we'll stride,

Hand in hand, with you, I'll forever confide,
Though our journey's direction remains unknown,
In your warmth and wisdom, my heart has grown.
An angel's grace, in your soul I've found,
In your love and kindness, my heart's unbound,
No matter the path that our future unveils,
With you, through life's storms, my heart prevails.

12. Eternal Echoes of Unrequited Love

In the shadows of my heart, a tale is told,

Of love unreciprocated, of a love untold.

For in the depths of time, our paths did cross,

But destiny's cruel hand, it bore a heavy loss.

A girl so wondrous, like a radiant star,

She captured my heart, from afar.

Her laughter, her smile, like the morning's first light,

Brought warmth and joy into my darkest night.

But alas, she loves me not, or so she claims,

In her heart, another's name remains.

A man who treats her poorly, who fails to see,

The treasure that she is, the beauty she can be.

I long to protect her, to be by her side,

To chase away the tears, to be her guide.

Yet, my love, she sees as only a friend,

While her heart clings to the one who'll never mend.

We've shared kisses, moments so divine,

Yet her heart, it's not truly mine.

For the love she seeks, it's not in my grasp,

And in this cruel truth, my heart does clasp.

I see the intentions of that boy so clear,

Yet she's blinded, unable to hear.

The depths of my love, she cannot perceive,

In my silent suffering, I can only grieve.

Today, my heart broke once more, it's true,
For I know not what else I can do.
To protect her, to guide her, my only aim,
But my love for her, it remains the same.
Though my heart may shatter, I'll carry the weight,
Of this unrequited love, a relentless, cruel fate.
But I'll always wish for her happiness and cheer,
Even if my love can never truly be near.
In the echoes of eternity, my love will reside,
A silent, enduring presence by her side.
For the love I have for her will never cease,
Even if it cannot find its rightful place of peace.

13. Echoes of Departure

In the shadows of our tangled past,
I stand alone, my heart recast.
If you choose to walk away, it's fine,
I won't pursue, I'll respect the line.
Through the storms and the starry nights,
I was the one to hold you tight.
In every situation, I was there,
A love that showed how much I care.
But if you decide to cast me aside,
The memories, I'll learn to hide.
You were the only one I ever kissed,
A bittersweet memory that I'll miss.
I thought I'd healed, moved on from you,
But yesterday's pain tore my heart in two.
Right now, I'm lost in anxiety's grip,
My shattered heart, my emotions, I can't equip.
So I implore, please set me free,
If you no longer want a place for me.
Stop this game of coming and going at will,
For my heart can't take this endless thrill.
And though my words may drift on the breeze,
I hope for an answer to put my heart at ease.
But if silence is the reply that's given,
I'll find a way to move on, forgiven.

14. Guardian of the Heart: A Promise of Friendship

In the realm of friendship, pure and true,

There's a bond between me and you.

You're the sun that brightens my days,

And your laughter, like a song, always plays.

But my heart aches when I see your tears,

For the pain you've endured through the years.

Your love, so deep and genuine, you give,

But his neglect, it's so hard to forgive.

In his eyes, your worth seems so concealed,

While your love for him is vast, unrevealed.

But remember, my dear, you deserve respect,

A love so pure, no one should neglect.

Your sacrifices, your enduring heart,

Should never tear your world apart.

I pray to the heavens, I send a plea,

To make your life a better place to be.

I promise to stand by your side, my friend,

To ensure your tears find their end.

I'll be the shoulder on which you lean,

Together we'll find a love pristine.

I'll make you smile, bring joy your way,

With each passing moment, every day.

You can eat freely, without restraint,

I'll cherish the moments, not a complaint.

In your messiness, I'll find beauty and grace,
In your presence, a comforting embrace.
For you're a treasure, beyond compare,
A friendship so profound, one so rare.
So let the tears dry and worries depart,
For I'll protect your delicate heart.
In your journey, I'll be your guide,
With love and respect, forever by your side.

15. Eternal Bond: Embracing Friendship's Promise

In the tapestry of friendship woven fine,

A tale of a bond that forever will shine,

Between you and me, a connection so true,

A steadfast alliance, forever we'll pursue.

Your heart, my dear, I've seen it break,

For love you gave, yet he chose to forsake,

The respect you deserve, he failed to show,

It's time for your spirit and strength to glow.

With every tear that dims your lovely eyes,

A piece of my heart within me dies,

Your love, so pure, so genuinely sweet,

He should treasure it, at your feet.

But, my friend, I see your pain so clear,

As you shed those tears, year after year,

I pray to the heavens, to God above,

To bless your life with boundless love.

I promise, dear friend, I'll be by your side,

In every storm, in every high tide,

No more tears will fall, you have my word,

With my love and support, your voice will be heard.

I'll bring endless smiles to grace your face,

In your heart, I'll find a special place,

You can eat freely, without a care,

I'll cherish your messiness, your joy to bear.

And remember, my dear, this truth shall stay,
No matter who comes, in your life's array,
My love for you, an unwavering light,
A friendship so strong, pure, and right.
Through the trials of life, we'll navigate,
With a bond so deep, nothing can separate,
For in your happiness, I find my own,
In the love we share, our seeds are sown.
So, let's walk together, hand in hand,
In this journey of life, forever we'll stand,
Through the tears and the laughter, side by side,
In our unbreakable friendship, we'll forever confide.

16. Love's Lament

In the realm of love, a tale unfolds,
Of a heart that weeps, its story told.
A bestie dear, in shadows cast,
Crying for a love that didn't last.
A boy, indifferent, unaware,
Of the depth of love, the heart laid bare.
He wandered through life, without a clue,
Of the feelings deep, so pure and true.
Your love, a beacon, shining bright,
But he, ensnared in the dark of night.
His eyes saw not the care you bear,
For a heart so gentle, a love so rare.
He loved with convenience, a fleeting flame,
Not realizing your heart's pure claim.
Your tears, my friend, like diamonds glisten,
Yet shed for one who doesn't listen.
But hush, dear friend, let not sorrow reign,
For in your heart, love shall remain.
I stand beside you, through joy and strife,
A steadfast presence in your life.
Don't waste those tears, so precious, few,
On one who sees not the love in you.
I capture moments, snapshots in time,
Of your strength and beauty, pure and prime.
Even if you push, try to divide,

I won't step away, won't leave your side.
In your world, through joy and strife,
I'll be there, a constant in your life.
So, wipe away those tears, my dear,
Let not the pain draw near.
For in your heart, a strength so vast,
And by your side, forever, I'll last.

17. Whispers of Love

In the soft glow of twilight's embrace,
Where whispers dance and shadows chase,
There lies a tale of beauty's grace,
In eyes that hold a captivating space.
With hues that rival the morning sky,
Her gaze, a melody that bids goodbye
To sorrows past, to fears untold,
In those eyes, a world unfolds.
Like petals kissed by the morning dew,
Her smile, a beacon, pure and true,
It paints the canvas of the day,
In colors bright, in dreams at play.
And as the gentle breeze does sway,
Her voice, a symphony at bay,
With words that weave a soothing song,
In every note, a love lifelong.
I marvel at the way she speaks,
Each word a treasure, so unique,
With cadence sweet, and rhythms rare,
In her voice, a melody to ensnare.
Yet amidst this beauty, so profound,
A humble heart, with joys unbound,
I stand in awe, in wonder's thrall,
At the mere chance to be her all.
So let the world its secrets keep,

In whispered winds and dreams that sweep,
For hidden in these lines of rhyme,
Is a love that transcends space and time.
And though the truth may lie concealed,
In every verse, it is revealed,
For in the depths of this poetic art,
Lies the echo of a loving heart.
So listen closely, dear friend of mine,
To the whispers of this hidden shrine,
For in these words, a truth resides,
That in your presence, love abides.

18. Hidden Depths

In quiet moments, when shadows fall,
I think of you, the one who stands tall.
With a heart so kind, yet hidden deep,
A mystery that others may not seek.
Your eyes, they sparkle, a gentle flame,
A warmth that calls, whispering my name.
Beneath the surface, where few dare to see,
There's a sweetness, a side reserved for me.
In the busy throng of everyday strife,
You hold your ground, living your life.
Some may see strictness, a guarded face,
But I see strength, and a touch of grace.
Your words can be sharp, your glance a shield,
Yet to me, your heart is revealed.
You share with me, what you keep from others,
A bite, a laugh, a moment that hovers.
Oh, how the world misjudges your ways,
Not knowing the gentleness that stays.
For in your presence, I've found a friend,
A bond so precious, that none can bend.
When you smile, the world seems right,
Even on the darkest night.
For in that smile, I find my peace,
A love that makes all worries cease.
You, who are strict and soft in turn,

Teach me lessons I gladly learn.
To stand my ground, yet be kind,
To see the good, to seek and find.
Your heart is gold, though few may know,
The love you give, the care you show.
To me, you're perfect, just as you are,
My guiding light, my north star.
So here's to you, with all my heart,
A bond so special, it won't depart.
For in this world, you're a treasure rare,
A friend, a muse, beyond compare.
Though words may fail to fully convey,
The depth of feelings I feel each day,
Know that in silence, my heart speaks true,
A whispered wish, a dream of you.

19. Unwavering Love: A Tribute to My Best Friend

In the quiet moments when you feel alone,
And shadows whisper doubts in a muted tone,
When the world seems cold, a silent gray,
Remember my words and what I say.
You think no one loves you, but that's not true,
For countless hearts beat just for you.
In laughter shared and tears wiped dry,
In the sparkle of stars that light the sky.
I see the beauty in your every flaw,
In the childlike wonder that leaves me in awe.
You may drive me mad, yes, it's sometimes true,
But that's the essence of loving you.
You're special in ways words can't define,
A rare gem that glistens, eternally divine.
If love were measured, a scale wouldn't suffice,
For my love for you would break it thrice.
In your quirks and mischief, your innocent glee,
I see a soul wild and beautifully free.
You're a kaleidoscope of color and light,
A beacon that shines in the darkest night.
When you doubt your worth, look into my eyes,
See the truth reflected, no need for disguise.
You're cherished, adored, in ways you can't see,
An irreplaceable part of this tapestry.

Through every frustration, each moment of ire,
Know that my care is a constant fire.
It burns bright and fierce, unwavering, strong,
A melody of love, an endless song.
So, when the world feels harsh and cold,
And you long for a hand to hold,
Remember my promise, this simple truth:
You are loved, beyond any proof.
In the chapters of life, through joy and strife,
You're my best friend, a light in my life.
No scale can measure, no words can define,
The depth of my love, endless and divine.
You're a treasure, a gift, a joy untold,
With a heart of pure and radiant gold.
So, hold these words close, let them be your guide,
In you, dear friend, I take infinite pride.

www.ingramcontent.com/pod-product-compliance
Lightning Source LLC
Chambersburg PA
CBHW031248130726
47988CB00008B/3300